Interfacing Risk and Earned Value Management

Association for Project Management

Association for Project Management
150, West Wycombe Road
High Wycombe
Buckinghamshire
HP12 3AE

British Library Cataloguing in Publication Data is available
ISBN 10: 1-903494-24-9
ISBN 13: 978-1-903494-24-0

Cover design by Fountainhead
Typeset by RefineCatch Limited, Bungay, Suffolk
Printed by Latimer Trend and Company
Copy editor: Merle Read
Proofreader: Stephen York
Publishing Manager: Ingmar Folkmans

Contents

Contents

Contributors

Dave Boden	Quintec
Lauren Bone	Bone Consulting Ltd
Peter Campbell	APM Risk SIG
David Chard	BAE Systems
Edwina Hayward	BMT Sigma Ltd
David Hillson	Risk Doctor & Partners
Val Jonas	Risk Decisions Limited
Bob Llewelyn	Rolls-Royce
Pete Mill	BAE Systems
Ken Newland	Quintec
Kerry Smith	Ministry of Defence
Tom Teixeira	Rolls-Royce
Tony Welch	BAE Systems
Daniel Wynne	Turner & Townsend

Foreword

Increasingly project management has been compartmentalised into its discrete skill elements: product decomposition, planning, scheduling, cost estimating, requirements management, risk management and performance management techniques such as earned value management. Practitioners understand that this is done to further develop and enhance the value of these disciplines to the project manager, but specialising may overlook the interfaces that make the management disciplines a cohesive whole.

Since January 2005 a group of earned value management and risk management practitioners has been discussing how the individual practices of each could be enhanced by interfacing the two disciplines. The group has presented and shared interim stages of the work to EV and risk communities at UK and international conferences, which provided useful and encouraging feedback.

Has anything new been created in either discipline? Perhaps. Most importantly by sharing the disciplines and clarifying the interfaces, they better serve total project management: 'the whole is greater than the sum of the parts'.

I would like to thank the many professional organisations, companies and individuals who have contributed to creating and reviewing this guide. In particular, joint meetings and discussions with the USA National Defense Industrial Association Risk-EV working group have proved invaluable. This broad review has contributed to making this guide useful for practitioners, from a local and international perspective.

The journey continues. You are invited to test and evaluate the approach outlined in this guide. Feedback, positive or otherwise, on your experiences would be welcome.

Steve Wake, Chair APM EVM SIG

Acknowledgements

The following reviewers are thanked for their assistance.

Wayne Abba	Abba Consulting
Erkan Akar	PMI College of Performance Management
Abdullah Alqaed	PMI College of Performance Management
Lev Ayzner	PMP
Tim Banfield	National Audit Office
Mike Bartlett	BAA
Cheryl Baugh	Government Integrated Bus. Approaches Inc
Garry L. Booker	Project Frontier
Charles Bosler	PMI Risk Management SIG Chairman
Alex Bot	PMI College of Performance Management
Ann-Marie Byrne	OGC
Paul Close	Fujitsu
Anthony Corridore	PMP
John Cox	MoD Technical Enabling Services-PM EVM
Jonathan Crone	BAA
Al Delucia	PMI DVC Chapter
John Driessnack	MCR
Kevin Forster	BAA
Julian Foster	BAA
Stuart Gibson	BAA
Steven Godoy	Siemens
Danny Granger	Turner & Townsend
Steve Grimmett	Ball Solutions Group, Australia
Randy Harris	Pine Bluff Chemical DEMIL
Richard Hedges	CEO Ball
Arnold Hill	US Government Services Association Property Dev. Div. WPC
Martin Hopkinson	HVR Consulting Services
George Hopman	PMI College of Performance Management
Mike Hougham	Henley Management College
Dr David Hulett	Hulett & Associates
Shakir Khaja	BAA
Joe Knick	Washington Group International Inc

Acknowledgements

Dr Glenn Koller	PMI Tulsa Chapter
Graham Lovelock	MoD Technical Enabling Services-PM Risk
Emma Major	Major Value Consulting
Robert Marshall	PMI College of Performance Management
Gary McGifford	Turner & Townsend
Stephen Mercier	Turner & Townsend
Susan E. Meyer	Aero
Bonnie Moision	US - major defence contractor
John Moule	MoD Price Forecasting Group-PETTL
Lindsey Pilling	BAA
Nick Pisano	Safran North America LLC
Neil Porter	Australian Defence Materiel Organisation
David Pyle	BAA
Roy Robinson	Sympatico
Bill Sanderson	BAA
Ana Cristina Santos	
James Schuster	SI International
Harry Sparrow	NDIA PMSC
Prof. Steve Ward	University of Southampton
Patrick Weaver	Mosaic Project Services Pty Ltd
Dominic Wells	HVR Consulting Services
Sarah Wenn	BAA
Mike Williams	BAE Systems
LC Wong	PMI-College of Performance Management

Introduction

BACKGROUND

Earned value management (EVM) and risk management (RM) processes share a common aim of providing decision makers with the best information available when setting objectives and considering management strategies. However, they take differing approaches. EVM establishes project performance status and extrapolates that information to gain an understanding of future trends and the allocation of resource needed to successfully meet these objectives. RM looks to the unknown future to identify risks (threat and opportunity) and recommend early action to be taken to limit the impact and probability of threat occurrence or maximise the exploitation of opportunities.

Both EVM and RM are, in their own way, informing project baseline estimates by using both objective and subjective data. Estimating uncertainty can be reduced by comparison of data outputs from both disciplines, providing a better understanding of project progress and predicted future trends.

It should be remembered that this guide is not intended to explain either EVM or RM techniques; rather it assumes a level of knowledge in at least one of these specialities and moves on to outline an approach to make more efficient use of the captured data.

OBJECTIVES

Established project management methodologies acknowledge the use and benefit of control mechanisms to improve the setting and monitoring of project objectives. EVM and RM are two such techniques that have proven their worth, independently, in support of project control. However, there are areas where the disciplines are complementary that, if exploited, could bring added benefit to both disciplines and, therefore, to project management. This Guide seeks to show how data captured separately through EVM and RM processes can be more effectively utilised, identify where common or synergistic processes exist and increase understanding of how project management planning, monitoring and control can be improved through the integration of the two process.

This guide identifies the added value achievable when EVM and RM are combined in a project context (see Appendix B). It does not attempt to describe how to apply these techniques in a programme or business context, although many elements of this guide may also be appropriate at these levels.

The assumption is that the guidance here is undertaken from the start of the project lifecycle.

STRUCTURE

The sections presented aim to provide both RM and EVM practitioners with practical steps to follow, starting with how to establish the project baseline, followed by baseline change, analysis and decision making, and finally a section on the importance of culture.

Applicable working assumptions are stated at the beginning of each section.

The terminology used in this guide is compliant with recognised international standards, as listed in the glossary in Appendix C.

BENEFITS OF INTERFACING RISK MANAGEMENT AND EARNED VALUE MANAGEMENT

Potential benefits to be had from interfacing EVM and RM 'good practice', and hence the benefits to project management as a whole, are suggested in Appendix B, which identifies the improvement to RM from EVM good practice and to EVM from RM good practice. The ultimate benefits of applying EVM and RM practices are gained through delivering good project plans. These lead to better management of projects, which results in successful outcomes.

EVM relies on the establishment of a baseline against which performance can be measured in terms of schedule, resource usage and cost. However, this baseline must be agreed against a 'realistic' project projection that has been derived following rigorous risk-adjusted resource, budget and schedule estimating. EVM identifies a value for management reserve to be included in the overall project budget; RM provides the processes to derive this management reserve appropriately through rigorous risk identification and analysis.

The metrics used to gauge the success of applying a project RM process, whether for threat reduction or opportunity enhancement, are usually measured against the project's ability to achieve targets or milestones. However, in either case of threat or opportunity, the realisation is driven by implementing agreed actions and ensuring that these actions are actually carried out and monitored through the baseline change processes required for a robust EVM system.

Herein lies the key to EVM and RM interfacing: the recognition that added value can be found in both disciplines through commonality of purpose in setting, measuring and achieving project targets. A baseline that takes no account of risk is extremely unlikely to be achieved; similarly, risk response actions that are not resourced and effectively monitored are unlikely to produce the desired results.

1

Establishing the project baseline

INTRODUCTION

The following provides a high-level description of how to create a project baseline. The establishment of the baseline requires the following steps:

- Establish the project context.
- Develop the statement of work (SOW), initial work breakdown structure (WBS) and initial organisational breakdown structure (OBS).
- Develop a top-down budget and schedule.
- Identify the strategic-level risks.
- Perform the initial risk analysis (schedule and cost).
- Revise the top-down budget and schedule.
- Integrate the WBS/OBS to allocate appropriate scope responsibility.
- Create control accounts and perform risk analysis.
- Develop and update the initial performance measurement baseline (PMB), i.e. revise control account plans to incorporate agreed risk response actions.
- Update and baseline the project risk register.
- Agree the PMB and management reserve (MR).
- Approve the project baseline.

In practice some of these steps may be combined or tailored to suit individual business and project processes. For example, it may be appropriate for some projects to adopt the principles of this guide without applying the full rigour.

Each step is described in detail below, and Figure 1.1 summarises the steps in a flow diagram.

1

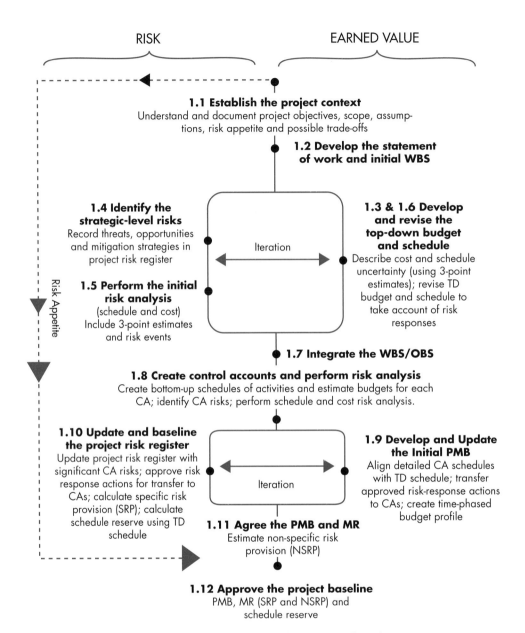

RISK

EARNED VALUE

1.1 Establish the project context
Understand and document project objectives, scope, assumptions, risk appetite and possible trade-offs

**1.2 Develop the statement
of work and initial WBS**

**1.4 Identify the
strategic-level risks**
Record threats, opportunities
and mitigation strategies in
project risk register

Iteration

**1.3 & 1.6 Develop
and revise the
top-down budget
and schedule**
Describe cost and schedule
uncertainty (using 3-point
estimates); revise TD
budget and schedule to
take account of risk
responses

**1.5 Perform the initial
risk analysis**
(schedule and cost)
Include 3-point estimates
and risk events

Risk Appetite

1.7 Integrate the WBS/OBS

1.8 Create control accounts and perform risk analysis
Create bottom-up schedules of activities and estimate budgets for each
CA; identify CA risks; perform schedule and cost risk analysis.

**1.10 Update and baseline
the project risk register**
Update project risk register with
significant CA risks; approve risk
response actions for transfer to
CAs; calculate specific risk
provision (SRP); calculate
schedule reserve using TD
schedule

Iteration

**1.9 Develop and Update
the Initial PMB**
Align detailed CA schedules
with TD schedule; transfer
approved risk-response actions
to CAs; create time-phased
budget profile

1.11 Agree the PMB and MR
Estimate non-specific risk
provision (NSRP)

1.12 Approve the project baseline
PMB, MR (SRP and NSRP) and
schedule reserve

Figure 1.1 *Establishing the project baseline*

WORKING ASSUMPTIONS

Definition of budget versus funds

Within an EVM system, the concept of budgets is different from the concept of funds. While a budget represents the cost performance target for a specific effort, funds represent the money available for expenditure in the accomplishment of the effort. Budgets are established for the relevant elements of the WBS and are time-phased.

Example: you budget for a house build totalling £240K taking 6 months; halfway through the project the estimated total build cost has increased to £300K, although the project scope has not changed. The extra £60k must be funded, but your budget does not change. You may revise your estimate to complete the project – funding forecast or estimate at completion (EAC) – to some appropriate value that exceeds £240K, but your budget still remains £240K. It is valid to change the budget only if you add scope to the house build, for example by including an extra bedroom or a garage.

1.1 ESTABLISHING THE PROJECT CONTEXT

This is the first stage in establishing the project baseline. It is important to ensure there is a thorough documented understanding of the project. As a minimum it should be possible to answer the following questions:

- What are the project objectives?
- What are the project requirements?
- What is the project scope?
- What are the project budget and schedule targets?
- What assumptions have been made?
- What are the possible trade-offs?
- What is your risk appetite?

Although the initial risk appetite is formulated at this stage, it will mature throughout the baseline process. Risk appetite is a determination of how much risk the project is prepared to accommodate in total, the level of confidence to be used to create baseline items, how much is to be held within the risk register and what risk exposure will not be supported by management reserve.

Tip: this information should be documented in either the project management or risk management plan.

   Output: documented project context.

1.2 DEVELOP THE STATEMENT OF WORK AND INITIAL WBS

The statement of work is a high-level statement of requirements, including deliverables for the project, that underpins the product-based WBS. This provides a structure for scoping the project, developing detailed budgets and schedules, and identifying risks.

   Example: the statement of work for the WBS in Table 1.1 is for a project to add a new garage to an existing home and complete all landscaping and other integration activity to present an appealing and functioning site. The scope includes all project management and facilities interfacing to the site.

   Output: statement of work and initial WBS.

Table 1.1 *Example WBS (based on Haugan 2002)*

WBS element	WBS description
1	Incorporate garage
1.1	*Project management*
1.1.1	Project planning & control
1.1.2	External permits & inspections
1.1.3	Project coordination & sub-contract management
1.2	*Garage*
1.2.1	Garage design
1.2.2	Foundations

1.2.3	Walls
1.2.3.1	Windows
1.2.3.2	Egress
1.2.3.2.1	Car door
1.2.3.2.2	Personnel door
1.2.3.3	Walls
1.2.3.4	Wall assembly
1.2.4	Roof
1.2.4.1	Structural roof elements
1.2.4.2	Weather protection
1.2.4.2.1	Roof covering
1.2.4.2.2	Gutters & drains
1.2.4.3	Roof assembly
1.2.5	Services
1.2.5.1	Electrical
1.2.5.2	Plumbing
1.3	*Garage integration*
1.3.1	Driveway
1.3.2	Landscaping

1.3 DEVELOP THE TOP-DOWN BUDGET AND SCHEDULE

With reference to the WBS and SOW, the top-down (TD) budget and top-down schedule are developed. At this stage these outputs exclude risk events, but they should include estimating uncertainty, using three-point estimates to describe optimistic, likely and pessimistic possible outcomes (see Appendix A1).

TD budget: this is an initial high-level estimate, against the scope identified in the project context, with budget allocated against elements of the high-level WBS (see Table 1.2).

TD schedule: this is an initial high-level schedule, proposing when the high-level activities are to be undertaken (see Figure 1.2). It includes milestones and logic links to represent interdependencies between the major elements of work.

5

Table 1.2 *Assessment of TD budget uncertainty*

WBS element	WBS description	TD budget allocation		
		Min	Likely	Max
1	Incorporate garage			
1.1	*Project management*	5000	5000	5000
1.2	*Garage*			
1.2.1	Garage design	1900	2000	2300
1.2.2	Foundations	4400	5000	6000
1.2.3	Walls	7500	8000	8500
1.2.4	Roof	8000	8000	9200
1.2.5	Services	2500	4000	4500
1.3	*Garage integration*	7750	8000	8500
Total			40000	

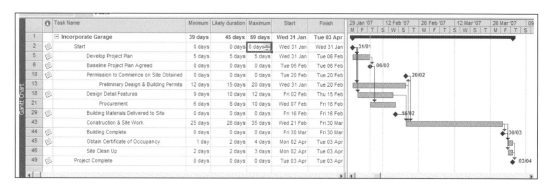

Figure 1.2 *TD schedule*

Tip: the schedule and budget structure may not be the same – for example, services may be identified as a single line item in the TD budget but may be distributed in different elements in the TD schedule.

Output: high-level schedule and initial budget allocation to WBS.

1.4 IDENTIFY THE STRATEGIC-LEVEL RISKS

Next, identify strategic-level risks to the project objectives, using criteria such as the risk breakdown structure (RBS) and risk assessment toler-

6

ances, thresholds and limits as set out in the project's risk management plan.

The aim is to establish a high-level view of the risks that are faced, and identify strategies for how these should be managed. Decisions on which strategies to implement will be heavily influenced by the organisation's risk appetite, alignment of stakeholders' objectives and related project strategic plans.

Example risks:

- Threat: as a result of recent changes in legislation, a significant redesign may be required to meet building permit requirements, resulting in increased cost and delay to the project. Avoidance strategy: escalate works to complete the design prior to new legislation taking effect.
- Opportunity: since the site adjoins several neighbouring properties, it may be possible to undertake some work jointly with one or more neighbours, allowing costs to be shared. Enhancement strategy: investigate possibilities with neighbours.

At this point the project risk register will contain strategic-level risks to project objectives, associated with issues such as technical capability and broad timescales. Options for addressing these risks are considered, including strategies for avoiding, transferring or reducing threats, and strategies for exploiting, sharing or enhancing opportunities.

Tip: strategies regarding 'make or buy' are typical examples of options to be considered. Trade-off strategies are identified to address scenarios where the expected effect of risk responses may not be achieved.

Output: project risk register, containing a strategic-level view of threats and opportunities to the project objectives, along with associated potential risk response strategies.

1.5 PERFORM THE INITIAL RISK ANALYSIS (SCHEDULE AND COST)

Cost and schedule risk analysis should be undertaken at this stage to understand the confidence of achieving the TD budget and TD schedule targets. This analysis should include both the uncertainty estimates (step 1.3) and the impact of risk events (step 1.4). This process will help identify the most sensitive areas of the schedule and budget, and the key risks to be managed. Further analysis should be undertaken to determine the effectiveness of implementing risk management actions.

See Appendix A for supporting information on risk analysis.

Output:

- confidence of completing on time and on budget;
- estimates of the possible extent of cost and schedule overruns (risk exposure);
- key risks to be managed;
- areas of the plan most sensitive to the impact of risk and uncertainty.

1.6 REVISE THE TOP-DOWN BUDGET AND SCHEDULE

The development of appropriate responses to treat high-level risks will have an impact on the TD budget and TD schedule that could result in a change to the statement of work and initial WBS.

Example: sharing repaving costs with a neighbour may require a rework of the schedule to accommodate the neighbour's preferred timing for the works.

The TD budget and TD schedule will be updated to reflect any changes, which should trigger a further review of the risk register and a rerun of the cost and schedule risk analysis. At this point the budget estimates and schedule are still at a high level, and have not been developed to the control account (CA) level.

Output:

- updated TD budget and TD schedule;
- revised project risk register;
- new risk analysis results – confidence levels, estimated risk exposure, key risks to be managed and sensitivity analysis.

1.7 INTEGRATE THE WBS/OBS

The OBS should by now have been established and a level of confidence in the WBS achieved. The OBS is integrated with the WBS to reflect how the project scope will be managed within the organisation. The alignment of the WBS to the OBS creates the responsibility assignment matrix (RAM), which provides the framework of control accounts by which the project will be managed. The control account is the point of management accountability for specific elements of WBS and also for managing the associated risks.

Example: control accounts will be created for WBS elements such as construction, landscaping, project management and design. A builder will be appointed to carry out construction; a landscape designer will be selected to complete the site works (driveway and landscaping). In this case the control account manager (CAM) may be the architect.

Output: revised WBS, OBS and RAM.

1.8 CREATE CONTROL ACCOUNTS AND PERFORM RISK ANALYSIS

At this stage a more detailed schedule and budget are developed for each control account, including the assignment of activity to detailed work packages and less detailed planning packages. If the control account contains an area of the plan that has been identified as one that is sensitive to the impact of risk and uncertainty (as a result of the initial risk analysis in step 1.5), identify risks and three-point estimates for the control account activities, perform schedule and cost/risk analysis, and approve appropriate risk response actions for inclusion in the control account baseline.

Tip: if the initial risk analysis in step 1.5 showed there is limited overall risk associated with this area of work, a three-point estimate for schedule and budget for the control account may be sufficient.

An amount of budget, taking account of estimating uncertainty (budget and schedule), is established for each control account (see Appendix A1 for more details). This will be used to form the EVM baseline (the performance measurement baseline). A conscious decision is made as to where the schedule target and budget should be set along the spread of likely outcomes for each control account. This will be the project's position on uncertainty, and will depend on how aggressive a target the management wishes to set, on the basis of factors such as the control account manager's track record and ability to manage uncertainty. These control account targets do not include risk events, which are covered by management reserve at the project level.

Output:

- control account or work package level schedules and budgets;
- control account schedule and budget confidence levels (based on risk appetite);
- control account risks.

1.9 DEVELOP THE INITIAL PERFORMANCE MEASUREMENT BASELINE

To create the initial PMB, further planning is now undertaken to the level of detail required to deliver the project. This involves allocation of resources (budget) to activities and inclusion of approved risk response actions.

Creation of the baseline schedule is an iterative process whereby logical interdependencies between activities within control accounts are identified (if they have not already been identified in the TD schedule), and the detailed schedules are linked to create the integrated project schedule (Figure 1.3). This is then compared to the TD schedule and any differences reconciled.

Tip: the risk analysis for each control account schedule is used to identify schedule reserve buffers that may be inserted into the TD schedule to align contractual milestone delivery dates. However, the PMB should be set with no inbuilt schedule reserve buffers.

The summation of all control accounts time-phased budgets (Figure 1.4) – and undistributed budgets – associated with the scheduled activities

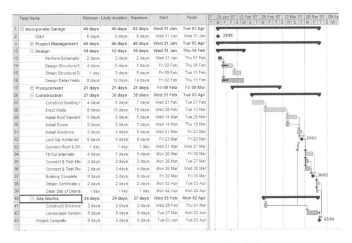

Figure 1.3 *Detailed schedule*

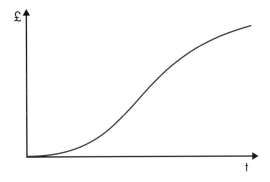

Figure 1.4 *Time-phased budget profile*

provide the initial bottom-up budget, to be reconciled against the TD budget.

Output:

- integrated project schedule;
- detailed schedule and time-phased budget baseline (initial PMB) reconciled with TD integrated schedule and TD budget.

1.10 UPDATE AND BASELINE THE PROJECT RISK REGISTER

The project risk register is now expanded to include significant control account risks (both threats and opportunities).

Management should review this project risk register and approve any further risk response actions (to reduce threats and enhance opportunities). Approved actions should then be transferred into control accounts, according to management's risk appetite, on the basis of appropriate risk analysis and cost/benefit analysis information. The residual assessment of each risk should then be approved (including projected staff and resources required to address the risk, should the risk materialise).

The specific risk provision budget is now calculated on the basis of the post-mitigation position of the approved threats in the risk register. Risk response actions in the risk register do not form part of the specific risk provision calculation. At the point they are transferred to the PMB they will be included in the PMB values, with the post-mitigation residual risk reflected in the specific risk provision calculation.

A calculation of potential savings can be generated for the opportunities in the risk register. This value should not be netted off against the specific risk provision. Any savings made by exploiting opportunities may allow work and budget to be removed from the PMB, e.g. because there is a more cost-effective way to deliver the same scope.

Schedule reserve is established by analysing the TD schedule (see Appendix A3 for more details), taking account of activity uncertainties (three-point estimates) and risk events.

Predicted costs arising from delays to the project (as a knock-on effect of a schedule risk reserve drawdown) will be considered and provisioned for within the specific risk provision budget, e.g. cost escalation of raw materials due to delay in procurement, or additional costs of maintaining resources for a longer period. Temporary schedule reserve buffers may be included in the TD schedule in order to set realistic milestones.

Output:

- the agreed set of risk response actions to be transferred to control accounts and an appropriately revised initial PMB;

- a set of opportunities to be incorporated into the PMB, with consequential threat that the opportunity is not realised included in the risk register;
- the baselined project risk register supporting the calculation of the specific risk provision required to recover from post-mitigation threats;
- the specific risk provision, including schedule reserve;
- the potential value of opportunities;
- a set of schedule reserve buffers used to set/protect milestones and estimate cost escalations due to schedule delay.

1.11 AGREE THE PERFORMANCE MEASUREMENT BASELINE AND MANAGEMENT RESERVE

The integrated project schedule is now established and forms the basis of the approved PMB.

Anything that has been identified as having a potential impact on the project but is not included in the PMB will be held in the risk register. The budget provision calculated and agreed for these will be held in management reserve. MR is composed of specific risk provision (for known threats) and non-specific risk provision (for emergent risks) (Figure 1.5).

Management will now estimate a value for non-specific risk provision, to cover emergent risks. This value will be based on management's view of the maturity of the information in the project risk register, the context in which the project is being undertaken, existing benchmark data and historic information on previous similar projects where appropriate.

It is important to designate authority for drawdown of MR. The specific risk provision is normally drawn down under the authority of the project manager. A decision needs to be made about where the non-specific risk provision is to be held. Whatever decision is made, it needs to be clear:

- that an agreed value of MR is under control;
- whether it must include management of emergent risk or not;

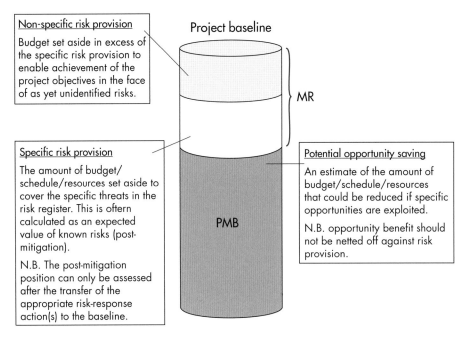

Figure 1.5 *MR = specific + non-specific risk provision*

- under what conditions additional project scope due to emergent risk can be accommodated, as EVM requires a capped value for the project budget against an agreed scope.

Tip: depending on the specific contract arrangements the ownership and handling of budget and risk provisions may vary.

 Output:

- approved PMB;
- approved MR budget (to manage specific and non-specific risk provision)
- potential opportunity saving.

1.12 APPROVE THE PROJECT BASELINE

The total budget and schedule for all authorised work (PMB), along with the management reserve and schedule reserve (see Appendix A), form the project baseline.

Output: project baseline.

2

Integrated baseline change management

INTRODUCTION

In this section we consider the impact of change on the project baseline components (PMB, specific and non-specific risk provision, and schedule reserve).

A diagrammatic representation of the integrated baseline change management process, encompassing risk review and implement transfer, is presented in Figure 2.1. This is part of the periodic project review process, but can also be triggered by unplanned events during the project.

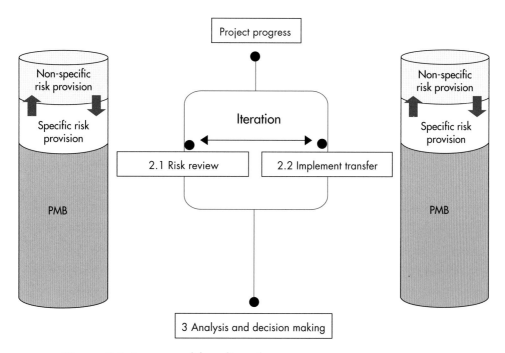

Figure 2.1 *Integrated baseline change management process*

WORKING ASSUMPTIONS

EVM guidance covers many types of baseline change; the ones most relevant to the interface between RM and EVM are likely to be the result of:

- rolling wave planning – this involves the control account manager planning work in more detail, re-evaluating existing or identifying new risks, and incorporating appropriate risk response actions;
- approval of risk response actions – this involves a change in scope to the control account that may impact on baseline resource and schedule. New work packages can be created and management reserve assigned or released.

Where there is insufficient project baseline budget or schedule to cover approved change, or more threats/fewer opportunities materialise than originally forecast, the project may go into over target baseline (OTB) and/or over target schedule (OTS) position. This scenario is covered in EV guidance and is not discussed here.

Scope changes originated by the customer are not considered; these would normally result in an amendment to the contract and project baseline.

Tip: in the scenario where the remaining work needs to be completely revised, the PMB, MR and schedule reserve all need to be revisited in accordance with standard process for establishing the baseline, as described in Section 1.

2.1 RISK REVIEW

Risk review at risk owner, control account or project level is carried out periodically as part of the overall project review process. It is used to identify new (emergent) risks, and to manage or close existing risks. Transfer from or into non-specific risk provision does not affect the project baseline (Figure 2.2). The result is an adjustment to the specific risk provision.

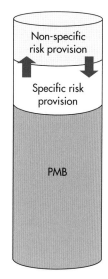

Figure 2.2 *Possible flow of budget between non-specific and specific risk provision resulting from a risk review*

2.1.1 New or revised risks

Drawdown from non-specific to specific risk provision arises when new risks (threats or opportunities) are identified or existing ones are revised as you gain more knowledge about the project.

The result is an increase in specific (and a corresponding reduction in non-specific) risk provision.

2.1.2 Closed or revised risks

Specific risk provision may be reduced when risks are closed or existing ones are revised. This arises when mitigation or exploitation actions are completed successfully, or when a key milestone is achieved and a number of risks expire.

The result is a decrease in specific (and a corresponding increase in non-specific) risk provision. Subsequently non-specific risk provision may be reviewed by management and a portion released to margin.

Tip: it is simplistic to think of the transfer occurring in 2.1.1 and 2.1.2 above on the basis of a change to a single risk. In practice, specific risk provision is always calculated as the budget required to cover the entire set of risks in the current project risk register, according to current risk appetite and based on latest risk analysis and cost/benefit analysis information.

2.2 IMPLEMENTING TRANSFER

Implementing transfer (work scope, schedule and budget) to or from the PMB is required when a new risk response action is approved or an existing one is discontinued, on the basis of a benefit analysis (Figure 2.3).

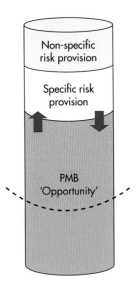

Figure 2.3 *Transfer of work and associated budget between specific risk provision and the PMB resulting from actions being transferred to and from the baseline*

2.2.1 Adding work to the baseline ⬇

A risk response action is included in the baseline to mitigate a threat or exploit an opportunity, or to recover from a threat that has occurred.

The result is an increase in PMB and an equal and opposite decrease in specific risk provision.

2.2.2 Removing work from the baseline ⬆

Work may be removed from the baseline when a risk response action is discontinued or when an opportunity is realised.

The result is a decrease in PMB and an increase in either or both of the specific risk provision (if a residual risk is introduced) and non-specific risk provision (where there is a difference between the budget released and any residual risk).

2.3 MANAGEMENT
OF SCHEDULE RESERVE

An authorised change request may result in drawdown of schedule reserve (Figure 2.4). This can cause approved changes to multiple control accounts, including those not involved in risk response activities.

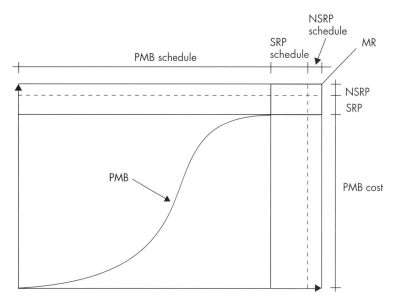

Figure 2.4 *EV graph with specific risk provision (schedule)*

Figure 2.4 details the time phased project baseline, breaking the management reserve into specific and non-specific schedule reserve.

3
Analysis and Decision Making

INTRODUCTION

Both the risk management and earned value management processes provide information to support managerial analysis and decision making. In this section, we consider how we improve this information by using a combined view from the two disciplines. In particular, we look at how to:

- calculate new estimate at completion (EAC);
- review EAC for specific risk provision (EAC_{SRP});
- review EAC for non-specific risk provision (EAC_{NSRP});
- calculate whole project EAC.

WORKING ASSUMPTIONS

Specific risk provision is based on threats only. Potential opportunity savings should not be netted off against threat provision. Both threats and opportunities need to inform management decisions separately because they are independent viewpoints (see Appendix A2).

3.1 CALCULATING NEW ESTIMATE AT COMPLETION

An EVM process uses various techniques to assess a revised forecast of final cost against the agreed scope in the PMB. Any such revised forecast is termed the estimate at completion (EAC).

Tip: just as the PMB was based on three-point estimates for activity budget and schedule, it is good practice to provide a three-point view of likely EAC outcomes, at the control account level. This provides the basis for a single-point EAC at the chosen confidence level. This process should address only estimate uncertainty, and not include any discrete risks. This may be compared to an independent three-point assessment at project level, as described below (Appendix A1).

The comparison of the EAC with the budget at completion (BAC), the approved baseline budget value, is used to inform performance, time and cost decisions. Initially, the EAC is the same as the BAC, but they will move apart if variances to the baseline budgets occur. Also, as the project progresses, MR is drawn down into the PMB, affecting the BAC value for approved scope changes such as those to mitigate and recover from risks, as described in Section 2. The EVM process generally allows only the BAC to change with change in scope. However, the EAC value provides an opportunity to predict a different outcome based on factors other than scope change.

In order to be accurate at project level, the EAC should be calculated not only against the PMB, but also for MR. It is only through the forecasting of both the PMB and MR that a complete view of the expected outturn of the project will be achieved. This will be obtained by considering the current forecast of risks on the risk register (the EAC for specific risk provision, EAC_{SRP}), as well as an evolved evaluation of the non-specific risk provision (EAC_{NSRP}), where it has been agreed this forms an element of the total project budget.

Example: the building work is now under way. The cost of construction materials has increased by 5%, affecting the current estimates in the PMB. The paving contractor has gone bankrupt (this had been identified in the risk register), and quotes from alternative suppliers indicate a likely increase in price and delay to commencement of that part of the works. All of these things contribute to the calculation of the EAC.

3.2 REVIEWING EAC FOR SPECIFIC RISK PROVISION

Specific risk provision is reviewed on the basis of the analysis of current risks in the risk register (new risks and existing risks) based on current risk response action activity already included in the PMB (see Appendix A for more details). Analysis is performed on the post-response assessment of the risks. This reassessed value takes into account current risk appetite and forms the EAC for the specific risk provision (EAC_{SRP}).

This risk analysis is rerun periodically and includes consideration and approval of any risk response actions that deliver a cost and/or schedule benefit. Approved actions (work scope and budget) are transferred to the PMB.

3.3 REVIEWING EAC FOR NON-SPECIFIC RISK PROVISION

As the forecast of specific risk provision is changed to reflect emergent risks, management may be required to consider also the revised forecast against the remaining non-specific risk provision. This will be determined by a re-evaluation of the original basis for justifying the non-specific risk provision budget.

3.4 CALCULATING WHOLE PROJECT EAC

$$EAC_{MR} = EAC_{SRP} + EAC_{NSRP}$$
$$EAC_{Project} = EAC_{PMB} + EAC_{MR}$$

While it is necessary to compare EAC against BAC at project level, it is important to realise that performance against each of the three component elements (PMB, SRP and NSRP) must be analysed separately (Figure 3.1). This is because each represents different management elements and will require a different management response.

- A difference in the PMB will be due to impacts that are already having an effect or are expected to occur in the future. The response will be to look for alternative efficiencies.

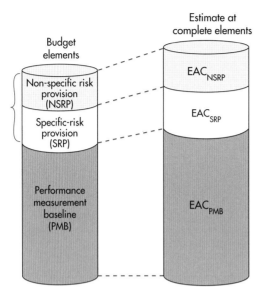

Figure 3.1 *Project EAC elements*

- A variance from the specific risk provision will be due to a change in the anticipated risk position. This could arise because more (or fewer) risks have materialised or emerged, or a key risk response action may have failed. Alternatively, a change in risk appetite may have resulted in more or fewer approved risk response actions (for example, management may attempt to exploit an opportunity).
- A variance on the non-specific risk provision may be due to a change in global or environmental effects, e.g. exchange rates. Under these circumstances the project manager may adopt a different approach to those elements that can more easily be controlled, such as the PMB and risk appetite.

Note: assessing the variance at project level does not imply that the variances experienced in each element should be netted off against each other. Negative variance in the PMB should not be offset by the transfer of MR.

If the resulting position (in overall project EAC) is unacceptable, then the project manager may propose the implementation of a trade-off option, as documented during the initial baseline planning steps (see Section 1). Any changes must be reflected in the PMB (according to change control outlined in Section 2).

4

The importance of culture

In this section we consider how risk and earned value complement each other, and also some of the cultural issues that need to be addressed in order to implement the two processes together effectively.

INTRODUCTION

Earned value management and risk management are complementary processes. Both are key aspects of the overall project management discipline. This document has described areas where the two processes can work together.

However, we should not overlook the human aspect of bringing two project management disciplines together. Typically RM and EVM disciplines have been exercised independently by specialists who are uncomfortable working outside their chosen area.

If the benefits of interfacing the processes are to be realised there must be:

- a clear process, with the interfaces between the two disciplines clearly understood and responsibility for the process elements clearly defined;
- a willingness by the practitioners of EVM and RM to better understand each other's disciplines as part of an integrated project control system;
- improved access to data and cooperation between the practitioners.

STAKEHOLDER RESPONSIBILITIES

Stakeholders should consider the following:
- Customer involvement is instrumental when developing a positive project culture. The customer needs to have a sound understanding of RM and EVM principles and data. An open and honest approach to

sharing the data appropriately will facilitate a mature environment whereby decisions are made on the basis of agreed and shared data. The relationship does, of course, go both ways: customers/suppliers will be asked to contribute data to EVM and RM Systems, and accordingly their data will be subject to similar reviews as internal company data.

- Management (both business and project) – it is important to the success of a risk–EVM approach that all parties are at a similar level of maturity with regard to each discipline. All involved should be encouraged to establish an open culture, so that poor variances, threats and opportunities can be raised and discussed without fear of criticism; there should be no hidden contingencies for threats and opportunities. Senior management must exhibit mature behaviour that demonstrates their commitment by applying these principles. The organisation should strive for a culture whereby lessons learnt from the past can be identified and incorporated into current planning activities.
- The project manager needs to ensure that the tools and techniques of each discipline are used during all project meetings. Risk and performance reviews should be incorporated into existing project meetings where possible as a seamless review of project activity rather than as separate process.
- Control account managers (CAMs)/team leaders need to participate fully throughout the EVM and RM processes, and have a broad range of expertise with competencies and capabilities in both disciplines. The CAMs need to assert ownership of both EVM and RM data. There also needs to be an understanding throughout the wider project management community of RM and EVM processes and their interactions.

KEY PRINCIPLES

The setting of the performance measurement baseline will reflect the company's current risk appetite. The assumptions made in order to set the PMB should be clearly documented and revisited during any subsequent revision or when developing an estimate at completion.

There should be an appreciation that the management reserve budget is expected to be used during the project lifecycle, and should not be seen as a source of profit. This should be understood by all stakeholders, including customers and senior management.

The project planning process used to establish the PMB should incorporate identification and management of risks and opportunities. The earlier that the organisation can be engaged in undertaking a harmonised risk identification/assessment and project planning process, the better.

When undertaking schedule risk analysis (SRA), the schedule network must be clearly related to that used for project control. Where there is a completely separate schedule network for SRA, the linkages between the two must be widely understood and accepted. They must not be seen as competing views.

The data/information for RM and EVM should be readily accessible to project stakeholders, in terms of both availability and understanding. It should not be limited to the realm of RM or EVM specialists. Ideally the information would be presented as a cohesive project position rather than separate EVM and RM views.

The whole of the project control community must be willing to step beyond their discipline. Management must support training to encourage this. This will lead to a more holistic approach to project management and improved project control.

SUMMARY

This initial guide has set out to establish the principles and potential practices for a closer relationship between the EVM and RM disciplines, and is considered by its authors to be both practical and appropriate. The authors believe that these principles can be used to develop and inform the advancement of organisations' risk and EVM capability.

APPENDIX A

Supporting Information

Here we consider what analysis is required to support risk management and earned value management working together.

Analysis is required during a number of steps in creating and maintaining budgets, as follows:

- calculating the amount of estimating uncertainty to include in the PMB;
- calculating specific risk provision;
- calculating schedule reserve.

The following sections deal with each of these in turn, explaining how analysis supports the budgeting process.

A1 ESTIMATING UNCERTAINTY IN THE PMB

Estimating uncertainty is calculated on the basis of uncertainty inherent in estimating any element of work (Figure A.1). The recommended way to generate the cost-estimating uncertainty is to estimate each item of work using a minimum, most likely and maximum value (three-point estimate) see figure A.1. Estimating should be undertaken as part of the earned value process. The analysis (for example, using Monte Carlo simulation) may be performed as part of the risk analysis process or as a discrete planning activity using standard risk analysis software.

When establishing the budget estimates for the PMB the range of estimating uncertainty should be assessed and a level of confidence chosen. This will be dependent on the project's risk appetite and will reflect how aggressive the PMB will be. On the basis of risk appetite, the estimating uncertainty is approved with a given confidence level. The budget values corresponding to this confidence level will now form part of the PMB and set the chosen target against which cost performance will be measured.

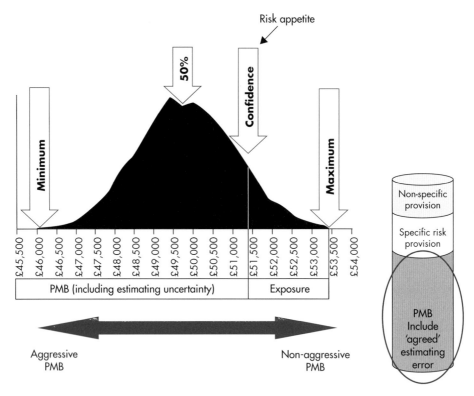

Figure A.1 *Analysis of estimating uncertainty (excludes risk events)*
© *2003–6 Risk Decisions, used with permission*

There is a chance that this estimating uncertainty will not be enough to cover worst-case scenarios. The amount by which you might overrun is called the estimating exposure. This exposure is not normally included in project budgets but should be understood and acknowledged by the authorising manager.

A CAM should be able to explain positive and negative variance arising from 'estimating uncertainty' on the basis of the confidence level chosen.

Note: care should be taken to ensure that risk events are not included in this analysis. Also, when choosing a confidence level, remember that the exposure to the right of that level may not be very likely to occur, but could have a large impact if it does.

A2 SPECIFIC RISK PROVISION (BUDGET)

Specific risk provision (budget) is generated from the analysis of threats in the risk register. Analysis is performed on the mitigated assessment of the risks, on the basis that approved actions are already budgeted for in the PMB. Specific risk provision does not include budget for opportunities. Both threats and opportunities need to inform management decisions separately because they are independent.

A simple way to determine specific risk provision is by calculating the sum of expected monetary value of each risk (Σ probability $\times$ impact). A simple view of risk exposure is gained from the sum of all the potential impacts. However, this may provide a distorted view of potential risk exposure, for example if the sample size is small, or the sample includes one large risk that overshadows the rest. In these cases the calculated specific risk provision is not representative of possible outcomes. A more informative picture is commonly generated using Monte Carlo simulation (see Figure A.2).

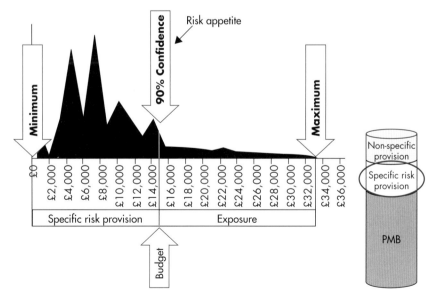

Figure A.2 *Monte Carlo analysis of risk events to determine specific risk provision © 2003–6 Risk Decisions, used with permission*

Risk appetite is used to determine the acceptable amount of risk exposure.

Note: a 'long' right-hand tail in the analysis shown in Figure A.2 indicates an overall risky position. It is common to think, for example, that the 90% confidence value will cover 90% of the cost of risks occurring. Figure A.2 shows that the 90% confidence will cover only about half the risk 'value', even though this should be sufficient in 90 out of 100 random samples; in the remaining 10 samples the exposure could be much higher.

A3 SCHEDULE RESERVE

As with budget, the time component (schedule reserve) needs to be established. This should take into account estimating uncertainty for activity durations, the estimated potential schedule impact of identified threats in the risk register and an allowance for emergent risks.

Consistent with the process for budget, analysis is performed on the mitigated assessment of the risks, on the basis that approved actions are already scheduled in the PMB. Schedule reserve does not include allowance for opportunities.

Unlike the approach to budget it is not recommended that values associated with estimating uncertainty and identified threats be calculated separately. This is because there could be multiple near-critical paths in the schedule that may not be triggered in separate risk and uncertainty models, but will be evident in the combined analysis.

The schedule risk analysis will enable decisions to be taken for establishing the PMB, top-down schedule, contractual milestones and specific risk provision, and will inform the values chosen for non-specific risk provision by providing details of the schedule exposure.

Here is an example of how the process might be undertaken in four steps. Details, for example of confidence levels used, may vary according to your circumstances.

1. Undertake a schedule risk analysis (including estimating uncertainty and identified threats).

2. Use the expected value to agree the time values to be included in the PMB (Figure A.3). Understand the level of confidence of achieving the expected values, which may be quite low.

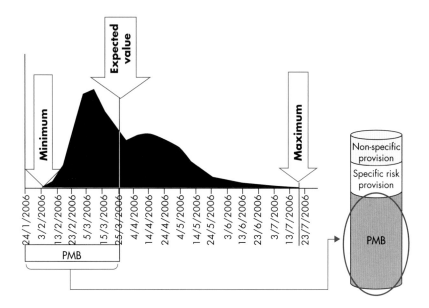

Figure A.3 *Schedule risk analysis to help determine PMB*
© 2003–6 Risk Decisions, used with permission

3. Agree a confidence level based on risk appetite (Figure A.4). The schedule risk analysis will provide the basis for determining the schedule reserve.

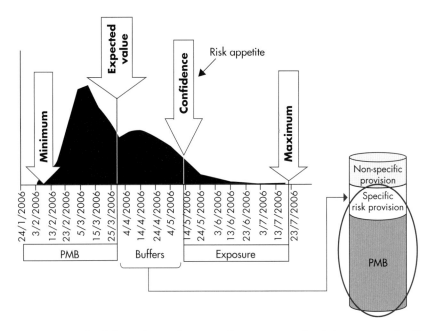

Figure A.4 *Schedule risk analysis to determine schedule reserve buffers*
© *2003–6 Risk Decisions, used with permission*

4. The schedule risk analysis will report the potential schedule exposure, i.e. how much the project might overrun. This, along with knowledge of similar projects, benchmark data and so on, may assist in determining an allowance for the schedule impact of emergent risks (non-specific risk provision).

APPENDIX B

Combined 'best practice' matrix

This table provides an overview of key activities undertaken within the EVM and risk disciplines, showing how good EVM practice supports improved risk management practice, and vice versa. The 'benefits to project control' column identifies the overall improvement to be gained.

Combined 'best practice' matrix

ORGANISATION	'Good' EVM practice	'Improved' RM performance	'Good' RM practice	'Improved' EVM performance	Benefits to project control
	• Preparation of OBS • Preparation of WBS • Definition of CAs • Development of RAM • WBS dictionary (customer requirements vs. work scope)	• Improved 'context' setting • Initial structure for identification of key areas of 'uncertainty' provided by WBS • Risk ownership defined through RAM development	• Structured identification of key areas of 'uncertainty' • Establishment of risk organisation, roles and responsibilities • Communication of 'context' within which risk is being managed (policy/strategy) • Stakeholder involvement in risk identification • Definition of risk appetite • Clear distinction between identified risk events and identified uncertainties	• Risk considered in approach to project – may change strategy • Management reserve approach, as opposed to 'blanket' contingency	• A combined (EV and Risk management) approach to project management should provide assurance that: • The performance measurement baseline (PMB) incorporates the entire agreed scope of the project • The work is scheduled to meet the project's objectives

	'Good' EVM practice	'Improved' RM performance	'Good' RM practice	'Improved' EVM performance	Benefits to project control
SCHEDULING AND RESOURCING	• 'Top level' assumptions defined • CA assumptions defined • Activities defined and CA schedules and interdependencies developed • Integrated schedule created and validated • Schedules resourced • Schedule baseline created	• Structured approach to facilitate comprehensive risk identification • Assumptions analysis • Schedule risks identified • Resource risks identified • 'Pre baseline' understanding of 'uncertainty' by customer and supplier	• Comprehensive risk identification and assumptions analysis • Joint (customer/supplier) risk register • Risk management process adequately resourced • Risk model(s) derived/refreshed from original estimates and risk analysis conducted (uncertainty and event risk treated separately)	• A more robust plan • Initial approved risk management activities can be accommodated by initial baseline • Common understanding of risk management strategy • Baseline planning and revisions informed by assumptions and risk analysis	• Risks are identified and managed effectively into agreed scope as required • Project level analysis of RM-based and EV-based forecasts will expose potential anomalies and inform better decision making at a strategic level • Integrated

39

Combined 'best practice' matrix

	'Good' EVM practice	'Improved' RM performance	'Good' RM practice	'Improved' EVM performance	Benefits to project control
BUDGET AND WORK AUTHORISATION	• Work descriptions finalised and authorisation documents created • Project baseline created (distributed and undistributed budget) • MR budget • Budgets finalised (reconciliation of top down and bottom up) • Budgets authorised • EVTs/PMTs established • PMB established	• Approved risk response activities embedded in PMB • Residual risk position understood • Disciplined approach to risk budgets • Process established for MR drawdown	• Structured/auditable approach to risk provision calculation • Risk management activity cost/benefit analysis	• Robust MR formulation • Predefined risk response and budgets • Process established for MR drawdown	management control processes are being maintained/implemented and developed where necessary

	'Good' EVM practice	'Improved' RM performance	'Good' RM practice	'Improved' EVM performance	Benefits to project control
SUB-CONTRACT MANAGEMENT	• Supplier plans agreed • Method of performance measurement and reporting requirements agreed • Contract terms agreed	• Framework for joint risk management • Agreement on risk funding	• Flow down of reporting requirements – lower-level plans support overall approach • Appropriate escalation of risk • Appropriate transfer/ownership of risk • Agreed setting/handling/authorisation of risk provision	• Managerial analysis and change control processes at the higher level improved/informed	
ACCOUNTING	• Well-structured/disciplined cost collection and accruals • Well-structured/disciplined update of schedule/progress • Calculation of earned value	• Framework for risk reviews • Auditable use and understanding of MR	• Auditable use and understanding of MR • Early warning of inadequate provision	• Early warning of inadequate provision	

Combined 'best practice' matrix

	'Good' EVM practice	'Improved' RM performance	'Good' RM practice	'Improved' EVM performance	Benefits to project control
MANAGERIAL ANALYSIS	• Update of forecasts (estimates to complete) • Critical path analysis • Identification of major variances • Review of interdependencies (impact analysis) • EV data/reports • Threshold/ variance analysis • EV trends and indices • MR review • Performance impacts review • Need for and types of change identified	• Update of forecast MR • Review of 'actual' risk impacts • Validation of forecast data • Correlation between risk exposure and experienced variance (data integrity check)	• Effectiveness of risk management activities monitored (spend vs. risk reduction) • Risk analysis refreshed (uncertainty and event risk treated separately) • Confidence in achieving targets considered	• Better informed EACs • Better understanding of the variances experienced and those that may occur in the future	

	'Good' EVM practice	'Improved' RM performance	'Good' RM practice	'Improved' EVM performance	Benefits to project control
CHANGE CONTROL (BASELINE MAINTENANCE)	• Structured baseline change request process • Disciplined baseline maintenance • Controlled use of MR	• Formalised approval of funding for risk response activities • Newly approved risk response actions/activities (scope and budget) embedded in PMB and appropriately monitored • Formalised cost/benefit analysis for risk response activities	• Formalised cost/benefit analysis for risk response activities • Controlled use of MR to fund risk response activities • Formal review and update of risk register	• Inclusion of risk response costs in EAC • Informs baseline change request process	
INTEGRATED BASELINE REVIEWS	• Formal reviews conducted • Baseline reviewed (work scope) and approved risk management activities included	• Independent assurance of risk identification and management	• Independent review of process and validation of risk data	• Identification and management of risk in PMB validated	

Notes. Risk management = threat and opportunity management throughout. To be read in conjunction with Glossary (Appendix C).

APPENDIX C

Glossary

TERMS

Term	Source*	Definition
Budget	APM EVM guideline	The resource estimate (in money or hours) assigned for the accomplishment of a specific task or group of tasks.
Budget At Completion	PMBoK	The sum of all the budget values established for the work to be performed on a project or a work breakdown structure component or a schedule activity. The total planned value of the project.
Change Control (Management)	PMBoK	Identifying, documenting, approving or rejecting and controlling the project baselines.
Control Account (CA)	APM EVM guideline	A management control point at which actual costs can be accumulated and compared to earned value and budgets (resource plans) for management control purposes. A control account is a natural management point for budget/schedule planning and control since it represents the work assigned to one responsible organisational element on one *work breakdown structure* element.
Cost/Benefit Analysis	APM EV/Risk Working Group	The comparison of costs before and after taking an action, in order to establish the saving achieved by carrying out that action.
Cost/Risk Analysis (CRA)	(PRAM)	Assessment and synthesis of the cost risks and/or estimating uncertainties affecting the project to gain an understanding of their individual significance and their combined impact on the project's objectives, to determine a range of likely outcomes for project cost.
Earned Value Technique (EVT) (or Performance Measurement Type, PMT)	APM EVM guideline	The technique used to quantify the budget value of work achieved.

(Continued on following page)

Term	Source*	Definition
Estimate At Completion (EAC)	PMBoK	The expected total cost of a schedule activity, a *work breakdown structure* component, or the project when the defined scope of work will be completed. EAC is equal to the actual cost plus the *estimate to complete* for all of the remaining work. The EAC may be calculated on the basis of performance to date, or estimated by the project team using factors such as impact of approved corrective actions, risk management activities/ actions, known downstream problems and best estimate to complete remaining work, in which case it is often referred to as the latest revised estimate.
Estimate To Complete (ETC)	PMBoK	The expected cost needed to complete all the remaining work for a schedule activity, work breakdown structure component or the project.
Funding	APM EVM guideline	The actual money available for expenditure in the achievement of contract work.
Issue	APM EV/Risk Working Group	A certain event associated with the contracted scope of work. Where the event impacts can be adequately quantified, they may be incorporated in the PMB; if not, an allowance may be made in *management reserve*. The allowance must be justified and supported by a three-point estimate. Some organisations may prefer to treat 'issues' as 100% risks.
Management Reserve (MR)	APM EV/Risk Working Group	This may be subdivided into: • *specific risk provision* to manage identifiable and specific risks • *non-specific risk provision* to manage emergent risks • *issues provision*.
Non-Specific Risk Provision (NSRP)	APM EV/Risk Working Group	The amount of budget/schedule/resources set aside to cover the impact of emergent risks, should they occur.
Opportunity	PRAM	An 'upside', beneficial *risk event*.
Organisational Breakdown Structure (OBS)	APM EV/Risk Working Group	A hierarchical structure established to identify the management responsibility for scope, schedule, budget and performance.

Term	Source*	Definition
Performance Measurement	APM EV/Risk Working Group	The objective measurement of progress against the *performance measurement baseline* (PMB).
Performance Measurement Baseline (PMB)	(PMBoK)	An approved, integrated scope/schedule/budget plan for the project work, with which project execution is compared, to measure and manage performance.
Proactive Risk Response	(PRAM)	An action or set of actions intended to reduce the probability or impact of a threat, or increase the probability or impact of an opportunity. If approved such actions are carried out in advance of the occurrence of the risk. They are funded from the project budget. Compare *reactive risk response*.
Project Baseline	APM EV/Risk Working Group	The total budget and schedule for all authorised work (PMB) along with the *management reserve* and *schedule reserve*.
Project Control System	APM EV/Risk Working Group	The aggregation of the processes, tools, techniques, methodologies, resources and procedures to help control a project. The system may be documented in a project control system description. A PCS is a set of processes and the related monitoring and control functions that are consolidated and combined into a functioning unified whole.
Project Management Plan (PMP)	PMBoK	A formal approved document that defines how the project will be executed, monitored and controlled. It may be summary or detailed, and it may be composed of one or more subsidiary management plans and other planning documents.
Reactive Risk Response	(PRAM)	An action or set of actions to be taken after a risk has occurred in order to reduce or recover from the effect of the threat or to exploit the opportunity. Such actions are funded from *management reserve*.
Responsibility Assignment Matrix (RAM)	(PMBoK)	A structure that relates the project *organisational breakdown structure* to the *work breakdown structure* to help ensure that each component of the project's scope of work is uniquely assigned to a responsible person.

(Continued on following page)

Term	Source*	Definition
Risk Appetite	APM EV/Risk Working Group	The amount of risk exposure an organisation is willing to accept in connection with delivering a set of objectives (of a project or business initiative).
Risk Breakdown Structure (RBS)	APM BoK	A hierarchical breakdown of the risks on a project.
Risk Event	PRAM	An uncertain event or set of circumstances whose occurrence would have an effect on the achievement of one or more of the project's objectives.
Risk Exposure	APM EV/Risk Working Group	The difference between the total impact of risks should they all occur and the *risk provision*.
Risk Management Plan	PRAM	A document defining how risk management is to be implemented in the context of the particular project concerned. This may be contained within a *project management plan*.
Risk Provision	APM EV/Risk Working Group	The amount of budget/schedule/resources set aside to manage the impact of risks. Risk provision is a component part of *management reserve*.
Risk Response Activities	APM EV/Risk Working Group	Activities incorporated into the PMB, either at project initiation or via the *change control* process, in order to implement a *proactive risk response*. These are identified as part of the risk management process.
Rolling Wave Planning	(PMBoK)	A form of progressive elaboration planning where the work to be accomplished in the near term is planned in detail at a low level, while the work far in the future is planned at a relatively high level, but the detailed planning of the work to be commenced in the near future is being detailed as work is being completed during the current period.
Schedule	(PRAM)	The timing and sequence of tasks within a project, dependencies among tasks, and the project duration and constraints.
Schedule Reserve	APM EV/Risk Working Group	The schedule component of *management reserve*.

Term	Source*	Definition
Schedule Risk Analysis (SRA)	(PRAM)	Assessment and synthesis of the schedule risks and/or estimating uncertainties affecting the project to gain an understanding of their individual significance and their combined impact on meeting the project's key milestones, to determine a range of likely outcomes for project dates.
Specific Risk Provision	APM EV/Risk Working Group	The amount of budget/schedule/resources set aside to cover the impact of known risks, should they occur. It is not advisable to net opportunities against threats, and so a separate value is calculated for each.
Threat	PRAM	A downside, adverse *risk event*.
Uncertainty	APM EV/Risk Working Group	The spread in estimates for schedule, cost and performance arising from the expected range of outcomes. Often termed estimating error.
Variance	PMBoK	A quantifiable deviation, departure or divergence from a known baseline or expected value.
Variance Threshold	APM EV/Risk Working Group	Acceptable cost and schedule variations from the baseline. Typically, thresholds are based on either a value or a percentage of the budget. Thresholds allow management by exception, whereby only those packages with variances exceeding one of the thresholds must be examined in greater detail.
Work Breakdown Structure (WBS)	PMBoK	A deliverable orientated, hierarchical decomposition of the work scope to be executed by the project team to accomplish the project objectives and create the required deliverables. It organises and defines the total scope of the project. Each descending level represents an increasingly detailed definition of the project work.
Work Package (WP)	APM EV/Risk Working Group	An activity or set of activities within a *control account* representing a discrete element of scope (ideally an output) where budgets are established, resources are planned and performance is measured.

*Where source is in brackets, minor amendments have been incorporated to the original definition.

ABBREVIATIONS

APM	Association for Project Management
APM BoK	*APM Body of Knowledge* (published by the Association for Project Management)
BAC	Budget At Completion
BCWP	Budgeted Cost of Work Performed
CA	Control Account
CAM	Control Account Manager
CRA	Cost/Risk Analysis
DB	Distributed Budget
EAC	Estimate At Completion
ETC	Estimate To Complete
EV	Earned Value
EVM	Earned Value Management
EVMS	Earned Value Management System
EVT	Earned Value Technique
LRE	Latest Revised Estimate
MR	Management Reserve
NDIA	National Defense Industrial Association
NSRP	Non-Specific Risk Provision
OBS	Organisational Breakdown Structure
OTB	Over Target Baseline
OTS	Over Target Schedule
PCS	Project Control System
PMB	Performance Measurement Baseline
PMBoK	*A Guide to the Project Management Body of Knowledge* (published by the Project Management Institute)
PMI	Project Management Institute
PMP	Project Management Plan
PMT	Performance Measurement Type
PRAM	*Project Risk Analysis & Management Guide* (published by the Association for Project Management)
RAM	Responsibility Assignment Matrix
RBS	Risk Breakdown Structure

RM	Risk Management
RMP	Risk Management Plan
SIG	Specific Interest Group
SRA	Schedule Risk Analysis
SRP	Specific Risk Provision
TD	Top Down
UB	Undistributed Budget
WBS	Work Breakdown Structure
WP	Work Package

Bibliography

1 American National Standards Association/Government Electronics and Information Technology Association (2002) *ANSI/GEIA-748-A-1998 (R2002): ANSI Earned Value Management System (EVMS) Standard*, National Defense Industrial Association Program Management Systems Committee (NDIA-PMSC), Arlington VA, US

2 Association for Project Management (2002) *Earned Value Management: APM Guideline for the UK*, Association for Project Management, High Wycombe, Bucks, UK; ISBN 1-903494-03-6

3 Association for Project Management (2004) *Project Risk Analysis & Management Guide*, 2nd edition, APM Publishing, High Wycombe, Bucks, UK; ISBN 1-903494-12-5

4 Association for Project Management (2006) *APM Body of Knowledge*, 5th edition, Association for Project Management, High Wycombe, Bucks, UK; ISBN 1-903494-13-3

5 Australian/New Zealand Standard AS/NZS 4360:2004, *Risk Management*, Standards Australia, Homebush NSW 2140, Australia, and Standards New Zealand, Wellington 6001, New Zealand; ISBN 0-7337-5904-1

6 British Standard BS6079-1:2002, *Project Management, Part 1: Guide to Project Management*, British Standards Institution, London, UK; ISBN 0-580-39716-5

7 British Standard BS6079-3:2000, *Project Management, Part 3: Guide to the Management of Business-Related Project Risk*, British Standards Institution, London, UK; ISBN 0-580-33122-9

8 Budd, C. I. and Budd, C. S. (2005) *A Practical Guide to Earned Value Project Management*, Management Concepts, Vienna, VA, US; ISBN 1-56726-167-1

9 Chapman, C. B. and Ward, S. C. (2003) *Project Risk Management: Processes, Techniques and Insights*, 2nd edition, Wiley, Chichester, UK; ISBN 0-470-85355-7

10 Cooper, D. F., Grey, S., Raymond, G. and Walker, P. (2004) *Project Risk Management Guidelines: Managing Risk in Large Projects and Complex Procurements*, Wiley, Chichester, UK; ISBN 0-470-02281-7

11 Fleming, Q. W. and Koppelman, J. M. (2005) *Earned Value Project Management*, 3rd edition, Project Management Institute, Philadelphia, US; ISBN 1-930699-89-1

12 Haugan, G. T. (2002) *Effective Work Breakdown Structures*, Management Concepts, Vienna, VA, USA; ISBN 978-1567261356

13 Hillson, D. A. (2004) *Effective Opportunity Management for Projects: Exploiting Positive Risk,* Taylor & Francis, New York, US; ISBN 0-8247-4808-5

14 Hillson, D. A. (2004) *Earned Value Management & Risk Management: A Practical Synergy,* Proceedings of the PMI Global Congress 2004 North America, presented in Anaheim CA, US, 25 October 2004

15 Jonas, V. and Welch, A. (2002) *The Integration of Risk and Earned Value Management,* Proceedings of the 1st UK International Performance Management Symposium, presented in Bristol, UK, 3 October 2002

16 Jonas, V. and Welch, A. (2003) *Risk and EVM: An Integrated Approach to Handling Management Reserve,* Proceedings of the 2nd UK International Performance Management Symposium, presented in London, UK; 9 October 2003

17 National Defense Industrial Association Program Management Systems Committee, (2006) *Earned Value Management Systems Intent Guide,* National Defense Industrial Association Program Management Systems Committee (NDIA-PMSC), Arlington, VA, US

18 Project Management Institute (2004) *A Guide to the Project Management Body of Knowledge (PMBoK®),* 3rd edition, Project Management Institute, Philadelphia, US; ISBN 1-930699-45-X

19 Project Management Institute (2004) *Practice Standard for Earned Value Management,* Project Management Institute, Philadelphia, US; ISBN 1-930699-42-5

20 Solomon, P. J. and Young, R. R. (2006) *Performance-Based Earned Value,* Wiley, Chichester, UK; ISBN 0-471-72188-3

21 UK Office of Government Commerce (OGC) (2002) *Management of Risk: Guidance for Practitioners,* The Stationery Office, London, UK; ISBN 0-1133-0909-0

22 Webb, A. (2003) *Using Earned Value: A Project Manager's Guide,* Gower, Aldershot, UK; ISBN 0-566-08533-X